The
Poetry
King

SCHOP

MR. GREGORY SCHOP'S
THE POETRY KING.

THE SCHOP

Avery Peerson, I call upon Calliope for thee.
Why have you come to quiet the king of poetry?

MR GREGORY SCHOP'S
THE POETRY KING.

NEVER BEFORE IMPRINTED.

THE FIRST EDITION

2021

THE FELL TYPES ARE DIGITALLY REPRODUCED BY IGINO
MARINI WWW.IGINOMARINI.COM.

ISBNs:
978-1-94048611-6 (KINDLE EDITION)
978-1-94048612-3 (SOFTCOVER EDITION)

THE SCHOP

COMMERCE, MICHIGAN: AT WWW.THESCHOP.COM

MMXXI

ARe you the silver, pewter haired Patron
Of Song that lends out lyrics laden gold?

GOod Lady, perceive sonnets knifed and plays unread and forgotten,
I would pray thee breathe on its life in ways undead and unrotten,
As your touch so did bring me a bright dove birth,
As soar such so did sing thee a flight 'bove earth.

TABLE OF CONTENTS

ACT I.

*"I needest the Nine, those
bright flints of thine!"*

The Poetry King   3

ACT II.

*"It's unexplainable with earthly
things of water, wind, and fire."*

Nothing Can Be   13
Lucky Archers   14
A Whim   15
I Stare to Her in Solitude
    Untold   16
The Fifth   17
Two of Hearts   18

ACT III.

*"But you are more than silvery
shimmering treasure..."*

A Stone's Throw   21
For She I Climb   22

The Hidden Place   23
The Glistening   25
Swashbuckler's Song   27

ACT IV.

"So I will ascend on and sing..."

Ticker   35
No Sleep   36
Lullabye   37

ACT V.

*"Honeybees gold lone
gatherings or swarms-"*

No Greater Fire   41
Warrior Storm   42
Beauty Be Thee   44

ACT I.

"I needest the Nine,
those bright flints of thine!"

THE POETRY KING

NOt one, not two, not three, not four is fine.
God!
Return!
I needest the Nine, those bright flints of thine!

The warming wet water of hell hath risen high.
Only your sparks of heaven can ignite the tide
So that men of kind can walk the line
Of brotherhood filled with clarity of mind,
Can walk the land with feet that touch the sand.

No fears, no tears, leave behind the warnings o'
    the seers.
Fill me with the past, and present the world a hero
    who cares.
With pull one hundred times the moon, let him
Upon the waves, ride and stride to set ablaze,
A warning shaped of endless haze to set
The balance of the world safe from craze.
Not brutes say I, but beasts of beauty!
Fair is fine and fine is divine; this tale's the sign—

"—Shut

"–Shut up! Ur waste in are time width this thing,"
Says Avery Peerson panting, pointing at the king.
He preaches and reaches the mountaintop to topple:
"Sew donut get two cozy," says Avery to the Apostle
And Sovereign of Poesy.

Avery Peerson, I call upon Calliope for thee.
Why have you come to quiet the king of poetry?

"Know won wants a bite too no yore lose words.
Aye can reed and talk. Eye can spake and wrought.
That's god enough for me two lie in piece.
Fore get a boat weather oar 'knot taken
The rode' way word path is windy or four sake in.
Wee wood rather watch a pitcher or a seine
Then add time to go threw in a strait line."

But like a picture worth a thousand words,
Who will paint each one, brush each phrase,
And stroke our eyes back and forth across the frame?

With a thousand of them, I will sculpt this art
    called life!
I'll stay on this mountain, your bard, your scop.
To help us all see ourselves, our hope.

I am not dead.
I will not leave or die or fly.

Too

Too much to see, to do, to try.
Before I bid you bye
So must you learn to laugh, to cry.
And only then
You will find I've fled.

"Navy you mine! Aisle warship myself
Naught thine, without cares, gods, or pears."

Avery Peerson,
Undumb yourself!!!

Begone beetle-bug born below the bottom of my beautiful
berm beside my mountain bequeathed to me by those born
of these waters of Helicon where bees' honey brimmed from
babes' ears and laurel leaves and sticks and staves for these
claims will not hurt me. For I am the Lyrical Liege, and no
one will depose me of poesy until I am banished beyond the
borders of your ignorance brick and mortar world, wherein
once I am belabored from my body, free to bend words in
a bodiless basin of bliss.

Something is stirring.
The wind has blown its last blow.
The sky has fallen its last rain.
The clouds have snown its last flake.
I am on this mountain, I should know.
Not of arrogance, but known for sake

Of

Of sun, rain, ice, and snow.
I am the first and the last to see it come, to see it go.
Something is stirring say I, it must be so.
Something is stirring without having whirring.
The olden ages are no longer luring, they're blurring.

Rise new age on this page!
Let my words break the cage.
Billionaires, millionaires I scoff at your plight.
Build your banks, your bonds, your might,
Your teams, casinos, and buildings bright.
Construct your beautiful kites,
But without that wind you'll have no flight:
Because of a boy[1] dead on a beach, you must know,
The new age has come, and the old ways must go.

You say that I am over and I am dead,
But you are me and I am you
Because I carry on in your head.
Remember this is what I see, say, and have said.

Run child, fly and soar
All doors shall open and no door shall close,
And never return to this mountain until you have rose.

From this mountain I croon continuously
To Californians, Texans, Michiganians, and New Yorkers

---

1 Alan Kurdi 2012-2015

Across

Across the Atlantic to Londoners and from there the seven
    continents I will sing,
Me, the Poetry King.

Why be the torn, the forlorn,
When you are the hero-born?

I know who I am, who I was, and who I will always be,
But now is the finish, the final act, death and life, life
    and death.
I'm not God or the gods. I'm the between, the here,
    the there,
The golden thread that ties two knots on opposite ends.
It keeps the earth, the sun, the moon,
The musical spheres in motion, in tune.

I am the fire from that first father:
The Great Spirit.
I am the Great-hearted.
I am the Lamb.
I am Ecgtheow's son.
I am Pendragon . . .

I'm the warrior, the protector, the goodness that fights the
    fight without fight.
I'm the silence on the 11th month, day, hour, and night.
And you, you all are the listeners and
The singers of my tale. The poets, the bards,

The

The scops of my story, the epoch of my epic.
You bring the songs to us . . . passing the songs to each
    other.
It doesn't matter the setting or the landscape.
It doesn't matter the time or the age,
And it doesn't matter these new world-words paged.

Descend this mountain, Avery Peerson!
And don't ascend again, do you hear, Son?

If you try to suppress me, you will found
That I will remain on this peak, not ground.
Sadly sigh I, despite my shoutin'
You'll return to desires and yearnings
To climb again this mountain
Against my wishes, wills, and spurnings.

And yet you will never rise to see above the level of me,
Above level you will be above an under mountain sea.
You will rise yet only over sea you will be.
I am the top of the mountain above the level sea, you see.

And perch he, shall he like "Ozymandias," by Bysshe,
Too will he waste away as an ology, or myth:
Missing the truth
Like eye and eye
Tooth and tooth.

Our

Our roots and strength are our arts
We leave in the fall
And re-leaf in the spring,
But it's the fire that melts us together.
It takes the solid and melts it and melts again into an
    invisible wind.
We are all particles and parts that call each other.
So waft the flames higher
Past the spires!
Build it to burn as a choir!
Heat it until it's lionfire!

ACT II.

"It's unexplainable with earthly
things of water, wind, and fire."

NOTHING CAN BE

NO word or phrase
Can match your gaze.
No smell or presence
Can catch your essence.
No shape or letter
Can describe you better.
No number or figure
Can measure your vigor.
No pattern of lace
Can reflect your face.
No color of blush
Can create your flush.
No speed or mile
Can surpass your smile.
No embrace or brush
Can contain your touch.
No star beam above
Can shine your love.
Happy, sad, or moody,
Nothing can be such beauty.

LUCKY ARCHERS

WHy not knock this game and draw
Both beau belle lock aim and saw
And send each who means so much
More than wounded words of such?

What if these forbidden arrows
Fly like hidden sparrows
Strike the middle parts
Of their spindled hearts?

Vanes we'll learn and find
'twill pain burn and bind.
Better not loose the shafts perhaps
Than have deuce hearts collapse.

So let these pointed doublets
Release anointed couplets
Turning unstrung wooed misses
Into love sung trued kisses.

A WHIM

OFten I walk past your way
As your cocoa-colored curls sway.
I think to grab you by the waist;
Pull you close with wild haste,
But like Poseidon's quake, Zeus' bolt,
I stay straight and shake or stop and halt
...Am forced to miss,
Thus forbid the bliss,
Yet once I wish it comes to this:

We, two Earthly flowers christened Mars and Venus,
Chance a whim which wiggles and blurs between us.
A meddling notion pushes our petals in a swirling motion,
Waving our stems around as the whirling ocean.
Now aligned by antiquitical design our blush lips,
I crave beauty, your chocolate eyes, your flush hips
...Only to offer a wordless
Regret for my neglect, my remiss,
I share with you a shy, secret kiss.

I STARE

I STARE TO HER
IN SOLITUDE UNTOLD

Stare to her in solitude untold.
She gazes from mazy, misty guises.
I see her light and her beauty unfold
With lips pink as fire, she peeks, she rises.
Her kiss is a warm cloth on my cool cheek
Like a blanket she wraps me and covers.
A powerful person I always seek,
Two tides together doubling as lovers.
Her colors set best when her light must bend,
Too bright to face at yet too far away.
She comes and goes but she won't ever end.
It is rare that both she and I can stay.
I always hope she will return here soon.
She is my sun and I, I am her moon.

THE

THE FIFTH

THe leaves drop down to become dust,
But you stay grounded and in my heart.
Even coldness and frozen love and lust
Cannot crack or break our bonds apart.
The air may melt and blow us beyond
Yet we will weather the wind hugging tight.
It all heats up as our bodies burn, sweat, and bond,
Molding us together as a sun so bright.
These four match not your beauty or my desire.
It's unexplainable with earthly things of water, wind, and fire.
Only in a fifth of divine sight and listening
Will bring the world closer to your christening.

TWO

TWO OF HEARTS

He hand is thrown,
Folded hearts ungrown.
Draws made,
Game played.

Yet still nice to quip
With each deuce's flip,
How child 'wish it weres'
Are wildcard cures.

ACT III.

"But you are more than
silvery shimmering treasure . . ."

A STONE'S THROW

SHe found me at the edge of a brook
And gave me a mighty look,
Polished me smooth and clear
Then skipped me across the water there.
I sank to the bed where I still lie,
Never to be moved or ever know why.

FOR

FOR SHE I CLIMB

When the world's mouth howls
And its south face scowls,
Toward she I climb
As I waste from time,
Hoping to get a closer sight
Of her beauty and brilliant might.

Up-up the slopes I rise
Peak-peeking my guise,
Praying to get a glimpse of her sunlit lips,
Food and drink for me both bites and sips.
With ropes I pull and pine to clip you in,
You, that ancient Angelic seraphim.

THE HIDDEN PLACE

HEre I
Cry, I
Smile,
My spot awhile.

No one knows
But bucks and does
What or where,
I do there.

On a path of gravel
Through woods I travel
Walking on demented dreams,
Lamenting the closed unseen.

Beautiful ways and things I told her
Now blocked by rock and boulders
Keep secret the swamp's cretin swallow,
Hiding memories eaten hollow.

Forest fawns shy by who mirror silliness
Far too silent to hear her prettiness
On paths pushed broken dark and done,
Then trees open to grassy meadows alight with sun!

As I along fragrant towers
Go by gold and red flowers
The bees hum,
A Love lost of.

I pause for purples looming
But often brush by blues blooming
Unscented wishes,
Forgotten kisses.

Snakes turn to fairies
As they escape the prairies
Of my poisoned mind,
There a cure to find.

My thoughts unsaid
Trail out my head
For me to heal and face,
All at this hidden place.

THE

THE GLISTENING

W Hen life holds no soul,
I, in doldrums stroll . . .
Closer to my last puff.
O' yet was lucky enough . . .

Sown from sea and foam,

In a rare place . . . of missing and non-ness,
To wear her face . . . kissing the goddess.

Grown to love and roam,

Soaring to heights higher, unknown,
To Olympian mountains we've flown.
Rising, falling, shore to shore,
I gasp, "I've never been here before."

You mirrored me

Hale her in, no doubt,
And she, me out.

On

On a scallop shell:

So many sad rhymes in the dark of night
Yet she's always been there beyond sight.
I buried so much pain on the ocean floor
But I'll drink her eyes till the sea's no more.

A hush, a never-tell.

I cry, "She is gone!"
And now I must go alone, along.
My Sleep, my Wake,
My ancient Keepsake.

Sigh I, "But I will ever glisten her song."

Sown from sea and foam,
Grown to love and roam,
You mirrored me
On a scallop shell:
A hush, a never-tell.

SWASHBUCKLER'S SONG

ON our land of love we should've lain
Beforehand of dove seas of change.
Under the trees, talling towers,
Thunder impedes falling flowers.
O I wonder if we had stopped our pain
Upon those dropped petals of rain!

As ships we carry, crest and fall,
But our lips ferry best of all,
Like wind and seas,
Oceans and breeze.

The Sound sinks and floats you and me,
Bound synced notes A through G.
Yours, a panicked rapid repeater,
Mine, a mimicked with added meter,
But make no mistake
These hearts can break.

What

What started out as just a random risk,
Rose in danger with each tandem kiss.
What we longed for—a slight tryst
Became wronged or—a rightness.

Nay, I fear you push or shove
Away, my clear wish for love.

When the sea tangos two to mistaken foggy crags
Then the *we* can go to forsaken boggy hags.
And like light in the darkest aquatic cave
Or calm at the wildest psychotic rave
(And I say only thus as wind and wave)
Can *us* send my only heart, mend and save
Its lonely part.

Your beauty brings the shunned thrill of day
On winds' wings—once still and stay—
Turning molded clays and silted hues with kill of gray
To churning golden ways, gilted blues, and sunned spilled rays.

From landlocked prose cages we moved away
And poemed seaward as sages we loved that day.

Perhaps the drenchless desert dying of thirst,
Traps us senseless, desperate, crying and cursed
Where our lustful waters and fun curling montages
There are just dull daughters and son luring mirages.

I've

I've Christened dames and ships,
Kissed pains and lips,
Commanded clowns with quips,
Traveled town mains through hips,
But you are more than silvery shimmering treasure
Or any golden glimmering pleasure.

When you left this ship the mast cracked,
Leaving only memories of cities sacked.
As it happens I sail numb my limbs to shivers,
I captain a vessel of dumb timber and slivers.
My sails torn and shattered,
I felt forlorn and scattered.
The ship lost and directionless,
You, so perfect yet perfectionless.
Nay, shot plug or fothering sail, nor weak roping of planks
Can unsay, shrug, unbother or nail my heart's creaks
    and cranks.

No matter how beautiful the past it seems
Let it drift on a sunset sea of gleams
And night time rifts of moonlit beams
Sail forward on the dream of dreamt dreams
While the behind seeps between wept swept seams.

The

The farther I sail the closer you are to me, Muse.
A watery whirlpool of my woes and woos
Circles me, a twirl-fool, who knows he'll lose.
There's no nautical way to go or choose,
I'm a mutinous heart hung by noose.
It's gone astray
And it's sailed away
So come back to me and stay
So together we can lay.

One thing about the luff buccaneer is he's always there.
He catches stuff, creatures ugly and fair,
But will never get caught in a marriage snare
Unless he captures the love of Calypso's stare.
For her keeps thee
Not you who keeps she.
The sea she's calm in she
And Me I can be
That moistening droplet in her eye,
Watered brineded mind kicks and screams
Slaughtered line wind picks up maelstrom memes:
Blowing hales and favored turning winds
Growing sails with savored burning sins.
True to nothing more than the four winds
He comes and goes
blows and rows
Risks in his kiss

With

With every pitch and rock of the boat
Therein stitched words knock from his throat:

"I found beauty in thee
That drowned beauty in me;
Then I saw what Beauty sees.
The sea will mirror loss
As thee will mirror soul:
The love I'll ever know
I'll have let never go."

My eyes fed, brung flood.
The tides red, sung blood.
From coast to empty coast
I go as a ghost at most.
Now shallowed and swallowed
Both hallowed and hollowed
It had ceased in me;
Dead pieced I be
Bone,
A pirate
Alone.

ACT IV.

"So I will ascend on
and sing . . ."

TICKER

YOu took my little heart
Right from the very start.
Kept closed and under key,
You opened it for me.
Tinkered to tick and tock
You broke its complex clock:
Overheated, melted,
Depleted, unfelt.

NO

NO SLEEP

NO sleep no sleep,
Your Memory I keep
Twisting into my Mind
Three stanzas with rhymes.

Nothing can bend
Such Beauty on end
Neither can Time turn
Nor teach and learn.

Such a special sight to me
Even a blind Heart can see
No other edict I trust:
To Love you, wake, I must.

LULLABYE

When wrongs blow me into furls,
I lullaby songs of sleep in your curls.
Things of the day run and wither away,
One would say fun with her's a play.

The world might say nothing was right
And such as time she left my sight.
Beyond the curtain I try to be strong
And I try to move on and along.

But the moth can't go back
To that thoughtless worm's sack.
So I will ascend on and sing
About my time on a butterfly wing.

ACT V.

"Honeybees gold lone
gatherings or swarms-"

NO GREATER FIRE

WE call it fire because it
Flickers our feelings,
Mills memories,
And melts moments.

We call it fire because it
Brings light where it was once dark,
Warms that which was once cold.

Shakespeare mused of it
Milton learned sight from it
Wordsworth yearned for it
Dante burned in it.

Even as its color changes
In an orange-yellow-blue fashion
This fire is still hot
With power, pain, and passion.

WARRIOR STORM

Only so much time a lover's licensed line:
"Hurry be, Thy mine. O hear me, Me thine.
One chance to spy love, soar, be birthed and born.
Let's dance in the eye of the warrior storm!"

Only so much time the lonely so such chime:
"Climb this stalk and vine. No more talk and whine.
Embarkening clouds from harkening crowds.
Let's fly in the eye of the warrior storm!"

Only so much time to whisper under shroud:
"Surrender our parts to unwetted rains.
Flooded hearts with no stated stetted names.
Let's sigh in the eye of the warrior storm!"

Only so much time to ease and call out pains:
"Eyes bleeding memories of one embrace.
Watering seeds of beauty none erase.
Let's lie in the eye of the warrior storm!"

Only so much time to make my final rhyme:
"Lightning, thunder cross the earthly crust.
Frightening blunder, loss of worthy trust.
Broken clouds of may, might, must."

Choken words of love not lust:
"O let Me die
In the eye
Of the warrior storm."

BEAUTY BE THEE

THe tall sway of a tree—
All of nature to breathe—
Cold warm whispers or storms—
Honeybees gold lone gatherings or swarms—
Ocean maels goddess myths of doves—
Legend tales princess wisps of loves—
Be no wind else to curl see or care—
Thee, the world's melody I hear.

FINIS.

Nigh night far, you dream to flee, disappear,
Yet thy bright star in me beams day so dear.
Thou canst cloud beauty with blindness or fear.
"Heaven guide us like a sextant when clear!"

Only with age will wisdom's whinnying unicorn run,
Ponying from page till kingdom hath come.
Loved he too much as ill Midas to gold,
Above she to such as nil might so hold.

I love thee, knave as I, then loved thus well.
"Save its spirit with chivalrous bend I shall!"

-The Poetry King

Made in the USA
Monee, IL
02 June 2021